Iguanas

by W. P. Mara

CAPSTONE PRESS

MANKATO, MINNESOTA

C A P S T O N E   P R E S S

818 North Willow Street • Mankato, Minnesota 56001

Printed in the United States of America.

Library of Congress Cataloging-in-Publication Data
Mara, W. P.
   Iguanas/by William P. Mara
   p. cm.
   Includes bibliographical references and index.
   Summary: Describes the physical characteristics, habitat, and behavior of the iguana lizard.
   ISBN 1-56065-426-0
   1. Iguanas--Juvenile literature. [1. Iguanas.] I. Title.
QL 666.L25M36 1996
597.95--dc20

                                    96-20750
                                      CIP
                                      AC

Photo credits
Marian Bacon, cover, 6. R.D. Bartlett, 4, 14, 47. W.P. Mara, 17, 19, 22, 25. James P. Rowan, 10, 20, 26-45.

Table of Contents

Words in **boldface** type in the text are defined
in the Glossary in the back of this book.

Fast Facts About Iguanas

Scientific Name: Iguanas are lizards. They belong to a family called Iguanidae.

Physical Features: Iguanas vary in length from about 14 inches (35 1/2 centimeters) to about six feet (180 centimeters). Their tails are longer than their bodies. They have five toes on each foot with sharp pointed claws. Many tiny scales cover their bodies.

Reproduction: Iguanas mate in the spring or fall, depending on where they live. They lay eggs, usually in underground burrows. The hatchlings usually look like their parents, but some are lighter in color.

Daily Habits: Iguanas are active during the day and sleep at night. Some live in trees, and some live on the ground. Marine iguanas spend most of their time in the water. All iguanas like to lie in the warm sun.

Range: Iguanas live in the southwestern United States, Mexico, Central America, the West Indies, and South America. They are also found on the island of Fiji.

Habitat: Iguanas are found in many habitats. They live on islands, in rain forests, and in deserts. Iguanas rarely stray far from a permanent water source.

Life Span: Iguanas can live from eight to 30 years.

Food: Iguanas mostly eat fruits, vegetables, and leaves. Some iguanas also eat insects and small rodents.

Chapter 1

Kinds of Iguanas

Iguanas are creatures of the desert, the rain forest, and the ocean. There are many different kinds of iguanas. They have been on the earth for thousands of years.

The word iguana (ee-GWAH-nuh) comes from the Spanish word iguan. It means a large type of lizard. Iguanas are lizards. They are a part of the **scientific classification system**. The system can be thought of as an upside-down pyramid. Animals that are most closely

Iguanas have been on the earth for thousands of years.

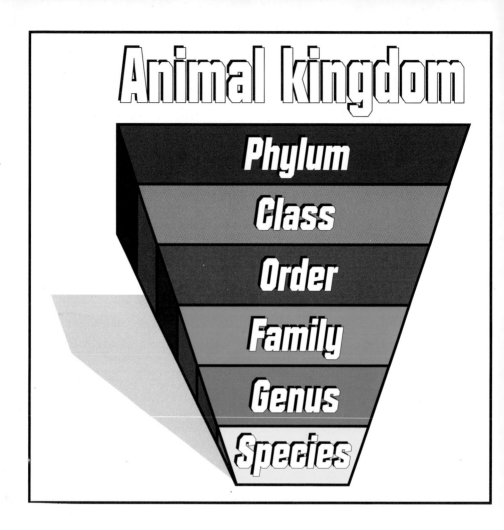

Animal kingdom

Phylum

Class

Order

Family

Genus

Species

related are at the bottom. The largest animal groups are at the top.

At the very top is a huge group known as a **phylum**. Iguanas belong to the Chordata phylum. Just below that is a **class**. Iguanas belong to the Reptile class. Then, there is an **order**. Iguanas belong to an order with snakes and other lizards. The name of the order is Squamata (skwa-MAH-tuh).

Smaller Groups

After that, there is a **family**. Iguanas belong to the Iguanidae (ee-GWAH-nuh-dee) family. There are smaller groups within the Iguanidae family. Each of these is called a **genus**. Finally, at the very bottom, is a **species**.

Each iguana has its own Latin name and English name. The Latin name is known as the scientific name. The English name is usually called the common name.

The common genus names of some of the iguanas are listed below. They are marine iguanas, Fiji iguanas, Galápagos iguanas, spiny-tailed iguanas, rhinoceros iguanas, desert iguanas, green iguanas, and chuckwallas. There are 700 species of iguanas.

Chapter 2
Where Iguanas Live

Iguanas are found in few parts of the world. Most iguanas live in the southwestern United States, Mexico, Central America, the West Indies, and South America. A few iguanas are also found on Fiji in the Pacific Ocean.

Most of their **range** is in a tropical zone. A tropical zone has high temperatures and high humidity.

Almost all iguanas are **New World** lizards. Think of the earth as being divided in half, from top to bottom. The half that contains North America and South America is the New

This marine iguana lives on Fernandina Island.

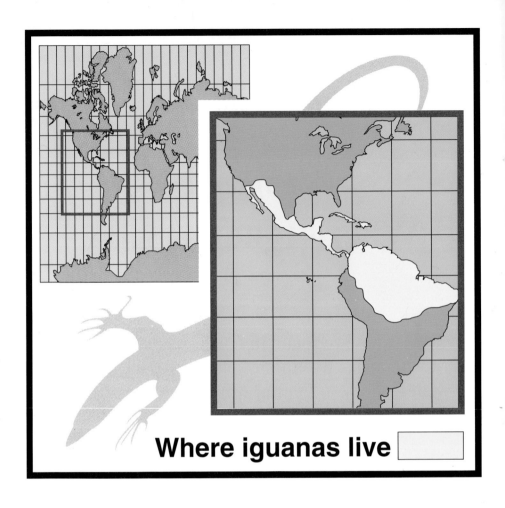

Where iguanas live ☐

World. The half that contains Europe, Asia, Africa, and Australia is the **Old World**.

Various Habitats

All iguanas have one thing in common. They all like hot weather.

But the natural **habitat** of iguanas varies greatly. Common green iguanas, for example, like tropical areas near water. They also like to be around a lot of trees. They are found from Mexico to the central part of South America. They also live on a few tiny nearby islands.

Desert iguanas, on the other hand, like dry, rocky places. They are often out searching for food during the hottest part of the day. They eat the leaves and flowers of the desert creosote bush.

Marine iguanas live in and around boulder fields. They are the only lizards that regularly feed under water. They live along the saltwater shoreline of the Galápagos Islands. The famous Galápagos Islands are home to many kinds of wildlife. The islands are in the Pacific Ocean. They are about 600 miles (960 kilometers) off the coast of Ecuador.

Chapter 3

The Iguana Body

Most iguanas are big. The common green iguana grows to more than six feet (180 centimeters) long. The smallest iguanas are the desert iguanas. They grow to about 14 inches (35 1/2 centimeters) long.

Different types of iguanas are different colors. The common green iguana usually is some shade of green. Some have dark-colored bands on their bodies.

Other iguanas usually are some shade of brown, green, black, gray, or dull yellow. Some iguanas have very pretty patterns. The desert

Some iguanas have pretty-patterned skin.

iguanas, for example, have a lot of dark gray and black spots on a light gray background.

Iguana Tails

An iguana has a very long tail. It is usually longer than the rest of its body. The tail has many uses.

The marine iguanas of the Galápagos Islands use their tails like ships use rudders. They use them to steer and propel themselves through water.

The common green iguana sometimes uses its huge tail as a weapon. It snaps it at enemies.

The tail of the spiny-tailed iguana has rows and rows of tiny sharp spikes. This iguana also uses its tail against enemies. It snaps it like a whip.

Iguana Feet and Heads

Iguanas have five toes on each foot. Sharp claws at the tips of their toes help them dig and

Iguanas' toes help them dig and climb.

climb. Their limbs are very powerful. They give iguanas great speed and jumping ability.

The head of most iguanas is long. It is covered with many tiny scales. An iguana's head can be pointy or rounded at the snout. Its ears look like little circles. They are just behind the iguana's jaw.

There is one eye on either side of an iguana's head. Iguanas even have a third eye on top. It is deep under the skin and cannot be seen from the outside. Scientists think this eye is sensitive only to light and darkness.

The head of most iguanas is covered with scales.

Chapter 4
Daily Life

Iguanas sleep during the night and are active during the day. This means they are diurnal. Animals that are active during the night and sleep during the day are nocturnal animals.

Like most reptiles, iguanas spend a lot of time **basking** in the sun. They do this because they are **cold-blooded**. They need the sun's heat to survive. Their bodies cannot make their own heat. Instead, they have to get their warmth from the sun.

Iguanas spend a lot of time basking in the sun.

Most iguanas eat fruits and vegetables.

Three Groups

Some animals are arboreal. That means they spend most of their time in trees and bushes. Other animals are terrestrial. That means they spend most of their time on the ground. Animals that live in the water are called aquatic animals.

Iguanas belong to all three of these groups. The common green iguana, for example, spends most of its time sitting on heavy tree branches. It comes down only to feed and breed.

Rhinoceros iguanas, on the other hand, prowl along the ground in the West Indies. They go into burrows when they are alarmed.

Marine iguanas spend their days swimming near the Galápagos Islands.

What Iguanas Eat

Most iguanas eat only fruits and vegetables. This means they are **herbivores**. Some young iguanas also eat small insects like crickets and grasshoppers. They are **omnivores**.

Iguanas get their food wherever they can find it. Herbivores find food in trees and bushes. **Carnivores** chase insects and other small creatures. They chase them along the ground, into burrows, and up tree trunks. Iguanas in the desert eat the fruits and the prickly leaves from cactuses. Marine iguanas chew **algae** off rocks submerged along the shoreline.

When they are thirsty, iguanas drink from streams or rivers. They also lick drops of rain or dew from leaves and branches.

Living Together

Many iguanas are known as colonial animals. This means they live in organized groups. Each group will establish a certain area as its territory. The group will defend its territory from all intruders.

When it comes to defense, iguanas can be fierce. They use their sharp teeth, long and pointed claws, and whiplike tails to fight enemies.

Iguana enemies include wild dogs and even humans. People eat iguana meat in Central and South America and the West Indies.

Run From Enemies

Like most reptiles, most iguanas would rather run from an enemy than fight. Iguanas that live near rivers and streams will dive into the water and swim from an attacker. Sometimes the fleeing iguanas will stay submerged for more than half an hour.

Other iguanas climb into trees. They go high so their attackers cannot get near them. Other

The chuckwalla burrows to escape enemies.

iguanas dive into burrows to escape their enemies. Or they slip under rocks or logs.

When the desert-dwelling chuckwalla wants to get away from an enemy, it jams itself into a narrow crack in a rock. Then the chuckwalla inflates its body like a balloon. It jams itself against the rocks to hold on tight. It is almost impossible to reach it to get it out. Native Americans would puncture the chuckwalla with an arrow to deflate it. Then they could remove it from the crack.

Chapter 5
Reproduction

Iguanas mate at different times of the year. The time that they mate depends on where they live. Those that live in the north usually breed in the spring. They breed right after a long winter's **hibernation**.

Those that live in the south may breed at any time of year. Most iguanas breed right after the **rainy season**. This often occurs during the fall and sometimes during the winter.

Often a male iguana will mate with a female only after he has had a pre-mating fight with another male. These battles can sometimes be fierce. The loser sometimes walks away with many cuts and bruises.

After a pair of iguanas have mated, the female will spend a lot of time basking in the

Iguanas get together when it is time to mate.

sun. This warms the growing **embryos** inside her. Iguanas lay eggs. They do not give birth to living young like many other reptiles do.

Laying Eggs

When the mother is ready to lay her eggs, she will dig a hole. After she has laid her eggs, she will fill the hole in again. This layer of dirt protects the eggs. Some iguanas dig their nest holes on little islands in the middle of rivers and streams. By doing this, **predators** are not able to get to the eggs and eat them.

Although most iguanas are big, the newborns are small. Even the largest ones are no more than one foot (30 centimeters) long. They are alert and feisty. The baby iguanas hunt down their first meals as soon as one day after hatching.

Female iguanas dig holes to lay their eggs in.

Scaly Head

Toes

Marine Iguana
Santa Cruz Island

Body

Tail

Chapter 6
Conservation

Some iguanas are rare in the wild. And they are becoming rarer all the time.

One reason that iguanas are becoming scarce is because of habitat destruction. A lot of the iguanas' natural habitat is being wiped out. In some places habitats are destroyed to make room for farms. In other places people are building shopping centers, hotels, and other buildings where iguanas once lived.

Groups Help Iguanas

There are, however, many **conservation** groups trying to help iguanas and other

It is rare to see an iguana in the wild.

animals. Laws have been passed that forbid the collecting of certain iguana species. And governments have marked certain areas as off-limits to hunters, trappers, and builders.

Scientists are breeding iguanas in captivity. Their work seems to be successful. Scientists and conservationists are making sure the iguana will not die out.

Zoo Trips

If you cannot view iguanas in the wild, visit a zoo. A zoo is a great place to learn about lizards and other animals.

Make the most of your zoo trips. Do not just walk around aimlessly. Leave knowing more than you did before your visit.

Take a notebook with you. When you see a lizard that interests you, stand quietly. Watch the lizard. See what it does. Then write down what you see. You can learn a lot about an animal by doing this.

Ask yourself questions. Is the lizard sleeping during the day? If so, it is probably nocturnal. Is the lizard in a cage by itself? Then

Look for the chuckwalla at the zoo.

it probably is a solitary animal and does not usually live in a group. How big is the lizard? What color is it? How does it act? You will be amazed at how much you can learn by observation.

If you can, bring a camera with you. A zoo is an excellent place to take pictures of animals. Lizards are beautiful animals. If you are a good artist, sketch pictures during your zoo trip. Photos and drawings of lizards give you visual reminders of your trip. You could

Look for the desert iguana at the zoo.

Look for the rhinoceros iguana at the zoo.

put the pictures in a scrapbook and use them later for school projects.

Some of the top zoos in which to view lizards are in Houston, Philadelphia, San Diego, and Washington, D.C. In Canada, two of the top zoos are in Calgary and Toronto. But there are many other wonderful zoos, too. Visit a zoo and enjoy yourself. Trips to the zoo are both fun and educational.

Some of the top zoos in which to view lizards:

Black Hills Reptile Gardens
South Highway 16
Rapid City, SD 57701

Calgary Zoo
1300 Zoo Road NE
P.O. Box 3036 Station B
Calgary, AB T2M 4R8
Canada

Houston Zoological Gardens
1513 Outer Belt Drive
Houston, TX 77030

Metropolitan Toronto Zoo
361A Old Finch Avenue
Scarborough, ON M1B 5K7
Canada

National Zoological Park
3001 Connecticut Avenue NW
Washington, DC 20008

The Philadelphia Zoological Garden
34th Street and Girard Avenue
Philadelphia, PA 19020

The San Diego Zoo
Park Boulevard and Zoo Avenue
Balboa Park
San Diego, CA 92103

The green iguana is one of the most common iguanas.

Glossary

algae—members of a large group of plants that do not have stems or leaves. They are usually green and grow mostly in water.

bask—lie or rest and enjoy a pleasant warmth

carnivore—animal that feeds on the flesh of other animals

class—group of animals or plants that have similar characteristics, ranking above an order and below a phylum

cold-blooded—having a body temperature that changes according to the temperature of the surroundings

conservation—the official care, protection, or management of natural resources

embryo—organism in its earliest stages of growth

family—group of related plants or animals, ranking above a genus and below an order

genus—group of closely related plants or animals, usually including several species

habitat—area in which a plant or animal naturally grows or lives

herbivore—animal that feeds on plants

hibernation—resting period during the cold winter months in which an animal sleeps and its body processes slow

New World—the Western Hemisphere

Old World—the Eastern Hemisphere

omnivore—animal that feeds on both plants and animals

order—group of plants or animals that are similar in many ways, ranking above a family and below a class

phylum—one of the larger groups into which plants and animals are divided, ranking above a class and below a kingdom

predator—animal that lives by capturing and feeding on other animals

rainy season—period of the year marked by rainstorms that usually are warm, heavy, and continuous

range—geographical area in which a particular animal can be found

scientific classification system—the way all living things are listed and categorized

species—group of plants or animals most closely related in the scientific classification system

To Learn More

Barrett, Norman. *Dragons and Lizards.* New York: Franklin Watts, 1991.

Chace, G. Earl. *The World of Lizards.* New York: Dodd, Mead and Co., 1982.

Coborn, John. *Green Iguanas and Other Iguanids.* Neptune, N.J.: TFH Publications, 1994.

Gravelle, Karen. *Lizards.* New York: Franklin Watts, 1991.

Ivy, Bill. *Lizards. Our Wildlife World.* Danbury, Conn.: Grolier, 1990.

McCarthy, Colin. *Reptile. An Eyewitness Book.* New York: Alfred A. Knopf, 1991.

Schnieper, Claudia. *Lizards.* Minneapolis: Carolrhoda Books, 1988.

Smith, Trevor. *Amazing Lizards*. New York: Alfrcd A. Knopf, 1990.

You can read about iguanas in *Reptile Hobbyist* and *Reptile and Amphibian* magazines.

This spiny-tailed iguana lives in Mexico.

Useful Addresses

**Charles Darwin Foundation for the
    Galápagos Isles**
National Zoological Park
Washington, DC 20008

The Long Island Herpetological Society
476 North Ontario Avenue
Lindenhurst, NY 11757

National Wildlife Federation
1400 Sixteenth Street NW
Washington, DC 20036-2266

Minnesota Herpetological Society
Bell Museum of Natural History
10 Church Street SE
Minneapolis, MN 55455-0104

Ontario Herpetological Society
P.O. Box 244
Port Credit, ON L5G 4L8
Canada

San Diego Herpetological Society
P.O. Box 4036
San Diego, CA 92164-4036

World Nature Association
P.O. Box 673
Silver Spring, MD 20918

This land iguana lives on Sante Fe Island.

Internet Sites

Herp Link
http://home.ptd.net/~herplink/index.html

Iguana Fun Page
http://www.io.org/~peelpgs/jim/iguana/
iguana.html

Iguana Magazine
http://www.infinet.com/~jax/iguana_mag.html

ZooNet
http://www.mindspring.com/~zoonet

Young green iguanas are beautiful.

Index